Like Horses
Jasmine Simms

smith|doorstop

Published 2019 by Smith|Doorstop Books
The Poetry Business
Campo House,
54 Campo Lane,
Sheffield S1 2EG
www.poetrybusiness.co.uk

ISBN 978-1-912196-26-5
Designed & Typeset by Utter
Printed by Biddles

Smith|Doorstop books are a member of Inpress:
www.inpressbooks.co.uk. Distributed by NBN International, Airport Business
Centre, 10 Thornbury Road Plymouth PL 6 7PP.

The Poetry Business gratefully acknowledges the support of
Arts Council England.

Supported by
**ARTS COUNCIL
ENGLAND**

Contents

For my English teachers

Like Horses

I too have stared like a horse over a fence
into the next field. I'm tired of knowing
that the wind up my nostrils is a sign of things
coming and going; have frozen from the inside
not knowing who opens the gate, or when.
I too have spoken the language of horse,
said things with my back legs,
caused offence, spoken too quickly,
turned out my upper lip after a taste of red wine.
I've run my hoof across the ground
just waiting. Now I know how to wait
like a horse does, knotting my mane in class,

looking very far into the distance, counting strides.
Sometimes I think I've come this far as a foal
sleeping with my head between my knees.
The only things I know for sure are real:
the sound of galloping, never to touch you
when your ears are flat back, how to get near you,
how to dream in the back of a horsebox,
how to fall, how to sleep standing up.

School

I wanted Boyfriends who were good at Science.
In Physics I drew love hearts, or bent and unbent
paper clips into the shape of love hearts. Whoever
doesn't know what love is hasn't been to a Physics
lesson and dragged a toy car across a desk to test
the forces on us. I tilted my hips and said "gravity
is the best man, girls, he never leaves", and rolled
myself across the carpet. First Kiss was a boy who failed
his Science GCSE and it was like being dropped into
a conical flask. Outside, life went on. Inside, I started
to believe in particles for the first time, crawled my way
back into the library, under a duvet. Physics Boy said:
"if you split an atom you find the world trembling
like a newborn". And then I stopped holding it together.

The Cult of Common Sense

We were everything you might expect
from a cult. Blue eyes, unbrushed hair
and Cheshire accents. By daylight,
farmers and builders. By night, afraid,
burning textbooks on planning law
in the garden of our breeze block home.

Only she was different. Always reading
indoors, watching the snowfall, forgetting
how to do simple things like tie a knot,
switch on an electric fence without feeling
the consequence, how to be a girl,
how to put a chicken out of its misery.

Which is why in the end we could not love her:
she was too much asking for permission,
too much wanting to be loved.
How she spoke like the women in books:
cold gets inside me whatever I do,
and I do not know what I do not know.

Hitching
For Lily

First piece of advice: forget instincts.
Learn by heart the Better Judgements

of an anxious world, the sensible
shoes and warm clothes, the impossible

distance between countries, like doctrines.
Far safer not to speak about religion.

Become good at small talk, so small
you could disappear in it, and do not

sleep in the back seats, eyes pulled shut
as though magnetised. Like how you slept

at the back of classrooms, the Judgements
rumbling beneath you like submarines.

Forget yourself. For small talk use only
the true facts remembered from Biology.

For example, that women blink more
than men. You try to catch his eyes

in the wing-mirrors. He says women
on the pill blink more than anyone.

You would put this down to sleepiness.
He would put this down to chemistry.

Second piece of advice: never disagree.
Every bad decision will keep us awake

in the next place. How we hitched our skirts
in the bathrooms, breathed bad words

onto mirrors. But this time you gallop
into sleep. You slide the doors of vans

like lifting the skirts of girls. You wonder
if you're dreaming when it starts to feel

like school again, the Autobahn dirty
and wide as the Humanities corridor,

the boys in the submarines singing.
And when your Mother tells it as the story

of the time you nearly died, you remember
it as the time you could not stop blinking.

Dear Tuba Teacher

I've studied and sweated and collapsed
inwards then outwards like a slinky for years
all so I can breathe like you, in circles.
I just loved how you could kiss people without
coming up for air, which was part of the attraction
for her – why she chose those lips, swollen
like pillows. We're known as the life savers
because it's true that no one can suffocate
kissing a tuba player. Just relax the lower back
then your shoulders, hips, and suddenly
all your limbs have fitted in: part of the biggest
and lowest sound in the world. I've copied you,
ready to go out with my gills showing
like diamonds across my collar bones, ready
to be kissed, to become a Prince, to pass into
the next life, where it's thought that a person
can ask no more from us than breathing.

At Hogwarts

Because we have magic
we do not have other things
like smoking and sex.

There is no nakedness.
No electric bells, blue light
from smart phones keeping us up.

No phones at all in the castle.
And because we live here
there is no start or end of days.

We're dots on a map. Look:
another boy escapes the dragon
on the playing fields. Look:

another girl dropped dead
in the bathroom.
I've broken all my bones again.

Every week I write
to the dead parents, *all is well*,
and every time it rains

indoors at breakfast, under
the imaginary sky. We suffer
from the weather.

Ofsted say we look unhappy
sitting here in the cloisters.
Still, we will save the world.

Gala

They'll be pulling out teeth on the bridge again.
When the band comes past, the noise
and the chaos is just enough to mask
the worst of it. The blood loose in the river.

I'm trying to imagine how much that hurts
by comparing it with my catalogue of pain,
some of which, it turns out, I barely remember
(though it surely must have been bad).

I suppose, as there's no good time
to be in pain, you may as well just get it over with
(this is my advice) while you're soft
and warm from the drink, like a woman,
your body in another man's arms
like a woman, this is my advice.

St Chad

Ordinary Durham Lad, hauled up
from the East Midlands to Aidens College.
An undetectable accent. A secret
library under his desk. His brother,
Cedd, also a saint, scored a hat trick
against George on the last day
of term. Chad has been our friend
ever since we started having boys
for friends. It's not been easy.
First, we couldn't get him to stop
touching himself in our bathroom.
Different definitions of sacred,
we said. Then he wouldn't stop
praying in the living room.
Then he wouldn't stop telling us
his dreams. Something changed us.
Now we keep a convent
in our student house. *Chad, we miss you.*
We who saw your elevation
outside Oswald's: the drunken angels
singing under the Cathedral's huge
shadow, the flashing blue light
that chose you, beaming you back
to wherever boys come from.

Patrick

When I woke up last night you were in my bed.
I've never been in bed with you
when you were alive. I was quite surprised.
I said you could stay as long as you didn't talk.
You said that was fine. You said you were tired.

Before I went to bed I'd been thinking
about your gap year in America
and your tendency to start conversation
but lose it somewhere, crashing in and out.
I can't be sure what you'd think of me now,
in my fake denim. I'm not even sure you'd think anything.

Recurring Dream

in which I am one of those born
without an oven in their stomachs,
who shout at themselves in mirrors.

Which is to say: the men. They are
all around me, hanging about under
extractor fans. An imposter, I stand

in the white coat of my ex-boyfriend
who we laughed at for taking Food Tech.
But this is a manly job, isn't it?

We wrap girls in tin foil, weigh
our hearts until they are light enough.
It's hard work. We move through tunnels

and end up in the underworld
which is an indoor place, but here
my brothers use their *outdoor voices*:

the sounds of manhood, filling
the backs of our minds
like hymn tunes. They let me in.

Heaven is a large, dark kitchen.
Fill your boots, say the men
at the table, this is all there is.

New Life on the Internet

It makes you uneasy, I realise,
that they send me friend requests.
How I don't accept or reject,
an old indecision playing up again
like a solar flare in the distance.

One girl has a profile picture
of a tree silhouette at sunset
in a blood-soaked field
and it makes me hear something,
a radio dropped down a well.

But the pictures come and go.
Like the herd last summer
(we kept our distance) I secretly felt
were not horses but unicorns.
They had flight instincts.

That was just the beginning.
I'm distracted by what they post:
prayers mostly. Lyrics in other scripts.
Flushed pink backgrounds. Some clichés.
Happiness. Happiness. Happiness.

How do you know this girl?
At the border I say three times
I don't know her,
which is absolutely the truth
though it feels like lying.

We don't remember how it started.
Some days I don't click anything
but drag the tiny arrow
(the user interface) hopefully
back and forth between objects.

And the fly we saw at the window
moments before take-off,
humming some old tune, a psalm,
pulls back again into the pink sky
three layers deep into the world.

Sandwich Artist

For Richard, comrade in oven gloves

There are times you would not even call yourself an artist.
Great moments of doubt, in which you reach
like a dancer for the next step, the oven door,
any space to put yourself in. These are the rough nights:
the empty cambros, the bad bread, when nothing rises.
The drunken chorus of critics who only want you
to succeed, to be beautiful. Who ask you questions.
Describe in words the sauce of the South West,
the purest shade of orange, of death and sex,
how to slice an onion into the cartoon image
of an onion. This is your current mood:
Brown, BBQ. An unrepresentable anger.
The weight of a drunk man's head in your arms.
They say Christ was born in a Subway
but you doubt you'd have noticed. Sometimes
you watch yourself on the CCTV, smoking
your first cigarette. You're not the person you were.
There's a church bell at 4am under a starry blue sky
and you've painted your house yellow.

Kingdom

It's true we forget what it was to be one
and so in a way they are aliens
though there's so many of them, it's hard
to think of them as hostile. In any case
they've already invaded. They're in your home
and your place of work and your church,
and without ever voting or deciding
you've furnished your life around them.
You say things you won't remember
and don't believe, just because you can
and you know how to, like speaking French
on holiday. You don't think of it as lying.
There's no such thing as lying to children.
There is no such place as France
but you take them there anyway
and teach them to swim because
most of the time there's only that tiny
undeveloped moment, over and over,
and we have to be trained to survive it.
You take photographs but don't print them.
There is no such thing as the kingdom
but you take them there anyway.

Testimony

I was 5 years old and in need
of a new school to hate.
They asked my Mother
are you Christian? This is a Church School
and my Mother said *no, but she is*
because I was always talking
to my friend Jesus in the garden.

Fair enough, by definition I was
a believer, so they let me in.
Always ten degrees weirder
than anyone could possibly expect,
I wasn't long in that place.
My friend Jesus was a regular guest
in the classroom, flipping tables.

Looking back, I don't remember
when we lost touch. I got older
and Jesus wasn't what I wanted in a friend.
Too unstable. The last time we met
in the garden, he was planning something big
and for once I didn't want in.
Can't we just be normal, Jesus?

I don't think he knew what normal was.
That was my first kiss, there in the garden,
and it was enough to make me realise
what I'm not: his girl, a believer.
I was 13 years old and in need
of something to hate that wasn't myself
and the devil said *come, my child*, and I did.

Wetherspoons
For Carrie

We joke that it's become our kink:
pretending to be old white men
nursing a pint (a soft drink).

We even do it on match days.
Gay culture is being curious
about the things that hurt us.

It's the Eve of Brexit. Is this it?
Gay culture is a veggie breakfast and chips,
nursing a pint (a soft drink).

There is no gay as in happy
but we're good here quenching our thirst,
discussing the things that hurt us.

There is no gay culture but us
realising we're in love on the brink
of Brexit, nursing a pint (a soft drink).

Then realising on the bus
that this is gay culture: to laugh
at the things that hurt us,
nursing a pint (a soft drink).

The Near Future

I suppose that where my parents live
could be the last place to gentrify.
Not because it's rough, but because
it's listed, and so far away from us.
When they reach my parents' house
(and by *they*, you know I mean us)
we'll have been back everywhere:
Turkey, Didsbury, Evangelical,
in and out of love via Luton Megabus,
the giant Tesco we always dreamed
of walking out to – four storeys tall
with a built-in Travelodge. The people
wondered about the Travelodge.
They couldn't see it coming. Soon
there'll be no place left not to go.
I heard it on the radio: there is such thing
as forced immunity from listing.
There is no more Megabus in Europe.
I call my Mother just to tell her this.

Acknowledgements

Thanks to the editors of the following magazines and anthologies; *Magma*, *The North*, *The Palatinate*, *Cuckoo Press*, *The Cadaverine*, *PUSH*, *Introduction X* (Smith|Doorstop), *All That's Ever Happened* (The Poetry School), *Something to Be Said* (Tower Poetry), in which versions of many of these poems were first published.

I am an eternally grateful graduate of The Writing Squad – a professional development scheme for young writers in the North of England. I have also benefited from the nurturing support of New Writing North, The Poetry School, Tower Poetry, the FOYLE Foundation and the Poetry Society. Finally, I thank my family and friends for this life that makes me want to write.